MIDNIGHT BAY

BY GAVIN BIGGS

ILLUSTRATED BY LORENZO SABBATINI

ABOUT YOUR BOOK

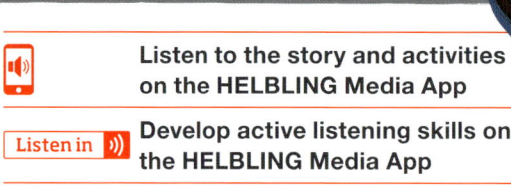

🔊	Listen to the story and activities on the HELBLING Media App
Listen in)))	Develop active listening skills on the HELBLING Media App
💬	Talk about the story
glossary•	When you see the red dot, check the word in the glossary
K	Prepare for Cambridge English Exams: A2 Key
e•	Go to ezone.helbling.com to do the activities

FOR THE TEACHER

e• Go to HELBLING e-zone for Cyber Homework, downloadable worksheets, answer keys and Reading Matters, the Teacher's Guide to using Helbling Readers in your class.

For a full list of both classic and fiction titles go to **helbling.com/english**

CONTENTS

HELBLING DIGITAL

INTERACTIVE ONLINE TEACHING AND LEARNING MATERIALS

THE EDUCATIONAL PLATFORM

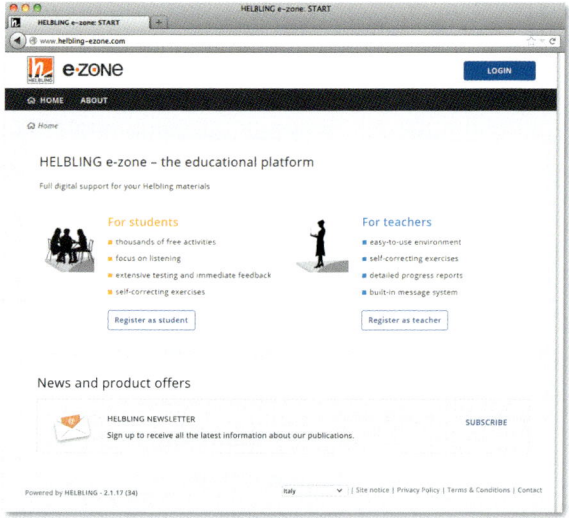

HELBLING e-zone is an inspiring new state-of-the-art, easy-to-use interactive learning environment.

Use the **personal access code** on the inside front cover of this book to unlock a host of self-correcting activities, including:

- reading comprehension;
- listening comprehension;
- vocabulary;
- grammar;
- exam preparation.

TEACHERS register free of charge to set up classes and assign individual and class homework sets. Results are provided automatically once the deadline has been reached and detailed reports on performance are available at a click.

STUDENTS test their language skills in a stimulating interactive environment. All activities can be attempted as many times as necessary and full results and feedback are given as soon as the deadline has been reached. Single student access is also available.

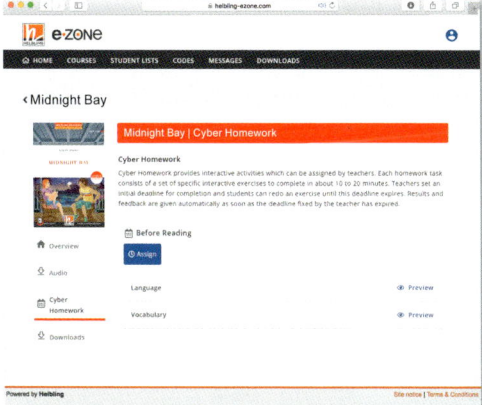

1000s of free online interactive activities now available for **HELBLING READERS** and your other favourite Helbling Languages publications.

ONLINE ACTIVITIES
ezone.helbling.com

helbling.com/readersblog

Love reading and readers and can't wait to get your class interested? Have a class library and reading programme but not sure how to take it a step further? The Helbling Readers BLOG is the place for you.

The **Helbling Readers BLOG** will provide you with ideas on setting up and running a Book Club and tips on reading lessons **every week**.

- Book Club
- Worksheets
- Lesson Plans

Subscribe to our **BLOG** and you will never miss out on our updates.

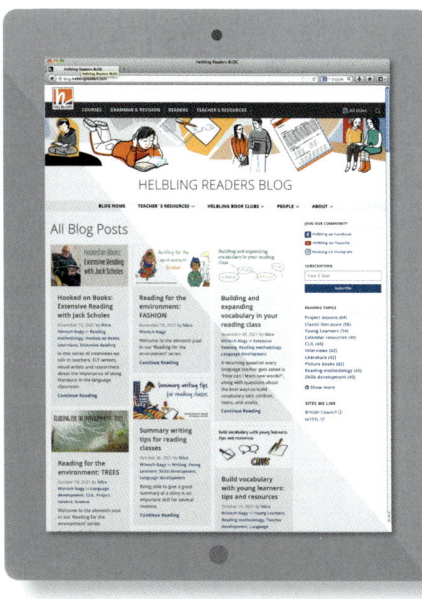

Listen in

Listen in is a new series of readers with a special focus on developing your students' active listening skills.

WHY IS LISTENING IMPORTANT?

Listening is key to **effective communication**. It occupies about 45% of the time we spend in communication. Significantly more than speaking (30%), reading (16%) and writing (9%)[1]. However, despite its importance, students say that listening is the most challenging of the 4 skills in English. The new Helbling Readers series, **Listen in**, aims to redress this imbalance by developing your students' active listening skills as they read.

> Over 60% of all misunderstandings come from poor listening, only 1% from poor reading[2].

WHAT IS ACTIVE LISTENING?

Listening and **reading** are often defined as **receptive skills**, because learners do not need to produce language to do them. While speaking and writing are known as productive skills. All skills are integrated and support each other in the process of learning, with students typically beginning with a receptive understanding of new language before developing a productive one.

Active listening is paying attention to a spoken text in order to fully understand the meaning of the words and the intentions of the speaker. Active listening helps students not only in their **learning**, but also in their **self-esteem** and **self-efficacy**. It teaches students to **communicate** their ideas and also to **think critically**. Plus, active listening promotes **mindfulness** and **empathy**.

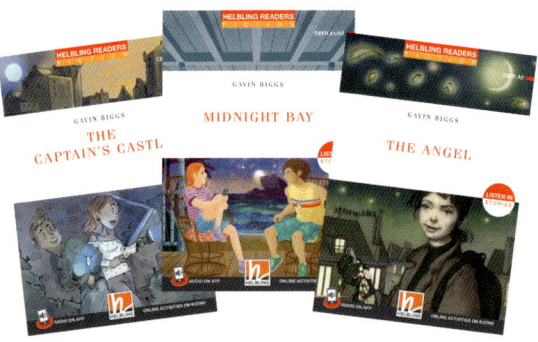

In the **Listen in** series, readers help the main characters to solve an exciting mystery by listening in to vital information and collecting clues. Active listening skills are developed through a variety of Before, While and After Reading activities.

Just look out for the Listen in))) box.

PRE-TEACHING KEY VOCABULARY

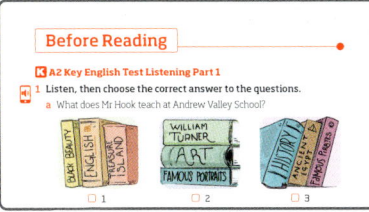

PRICELESS SWORD STOLEN!

📢 1 Listen to this news report about another theft from the Louvre Museum in 1976. Then answer the questions.

a What type of sword is it?

1 ☐ emerald 2 ☐ garnet 3 ☐ diamond

b In which year was the sword made?

1 ☐ 1824 2 ☐ 1924 3 ☐ 1976

Before Reading

🇰 A2 Key English Test Listening Part 1

📢 1 Listen, then choose the correct answer to the questions.

a What does Mr Hook teach at Andrew Valley School?

☐ 1   ☐ 2   ☐ 3

ACTIVATING BACKGROUND KNOWLEDGE

Special **Listen in** pages after each chapter develop active listening strategies and work on the following listening skills:

- Listening to distinguish words and expressions (discriminative listening);
- Listening for details and information (precise listening);
- Listening for general understanding (listening for gist and summarising);
- Evaluating and analysing (listening for inference).

Listen in

What is the voice on the TV saying? Listen, then do the activities.

📢 1 Listen and decide what the news report is about.

a ☐ The pollution from the car factory.
b ☐ The record-breaking colour of the seas.
c ☐ Tourism in Midnight Bay.
d ☐ A surfing competition in Midnight Bay.

📢 2 Listen again and write words that match the definitions below.

a people who live in a town or area
b shining
c the up and down movements of the sea
d people who visit a place on holiday
e place where large quantities of things are made
f don't think something is important

🌐 3 Go to HELBLING e-zone to do the activities and get a clue to help you solve the mystery of Midnight Bay.

My clue is

After Reading

DEBATE

LISTENING AND SPEAKING

Listen in and Speak and **Listen in and Debate** spreads take learners from attentive listening to critical response and help develop all-important **oracy skills**.

PRONUNCIATION PRACTICE

Throughout each book special **Listen in** boxes focus on **pronunciation**.

Listen in 🔊

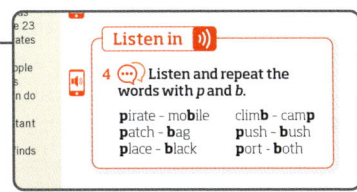

📢 4 💬 Listen and repeat the words with p and b.

pirate - mo**b**ile   **c**limb - cam**p**
patch - **b**ag   **p**ush - **b**ush
place - **b**lack   **p**ort - **b**oth

NOTES

[1] Raphael Ahmed for *The British Council*.
[2] Iwankovitsch, R. *The Importance of Listening*.

Under the sea

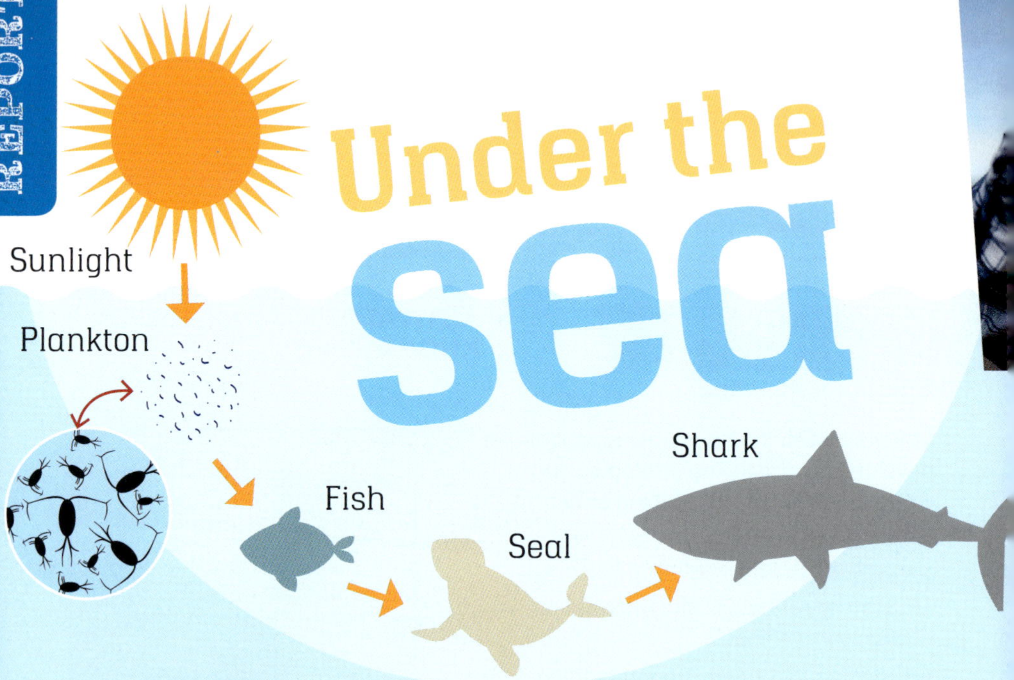

Sunlight

Plankton

Fish

Seal

Shark

Food chains

A food chain describes what animals eat. In the ocean, the animals at the top of the food chain are often large and fast, like sharks. But what is at the bottom? The answer is plankton. Plankton are microscopic• plants and animals that float• around in the sea. Plant plankton use the light from the sun to create energy. They are at the the start of the food chain. Then, animal plankton eat the plant plankton. And, in turn, the animal plankton become food for the marine food chain – fish, corals•, and even sharks! The whale shark is the largest fish in the sea and its favourite food is plankton.

Plankton power

Plankton may be tiny•, but they are very important. Plant plankton make 50% of the oxygen• on Earth. So we need plankton to breathe•!
And some plankton make their own light. This is called bioluminescence. When millions of tiny plankton glow• together, it makes the sea glow in the dark.

Working with water

Marine biology is the study of life in the sea. And people who do this are called marine biologists. They work underwater, on boats and in science labs•. They can study anything from huge• whales to tiny invisible• plankton.

- **breathe:** move air in and out of the lungs through the mouth
- **corals:**
- **float:** move slowly around in water or air
- **glow:** make light
- **huge:** very big
- **invisible:** that you can't see
- **labs:** laboratories where scientists work
- **microscopic:** very very small
- **oxygen:** the air we breathe
- **tiny:** very small

WATER WORDS

1 Listen to the marine biologist talking about his job. Then answer the questions.

a What type of boat does the marine biologist use?
  1 ☐ a dinghy
  2 ☐ a fishing boat
  3 ☐ a shipwreck

b What do the university students help collect?
  1 ☐ water samples from the sea
  2 ☐ fish from the coral reefs
  3 ☐ sand from the beach

c What does the marine biologist say is in Plymouth?
  1 ☐ a beautiful beach
  2 ☐ a famous surf school
  3 ☐ a Marine Biology Centre

Listen in))

Sea and *see* are homophones. They have different spelling, but you pronounce them the same way.

2 **Listen, then repeat the sentence.**
And I can't wait to see all the sea animals that you have here!

3 Match the homophones, then listen and check.

a ☐ ate	**1** high
b ☐ bye	**2** whole
c ☐ hole	**3** eight
d ☐ hi	**4** buy

MIDNIGHT BAY

☐ Don Montero

☐ Sandra Montes

☐ Bull

☐ Mako

1 Listen and decide who is speaking. Write the letters beside the pictures.

2 Look at the pictures and find someone:

a wearing a police uniform,
b with tattoos,
c wearing an expensive suit,
d who is a professor,
e who is from Bristol in England.

3 Share your answers to Exercise 2 with a friend.

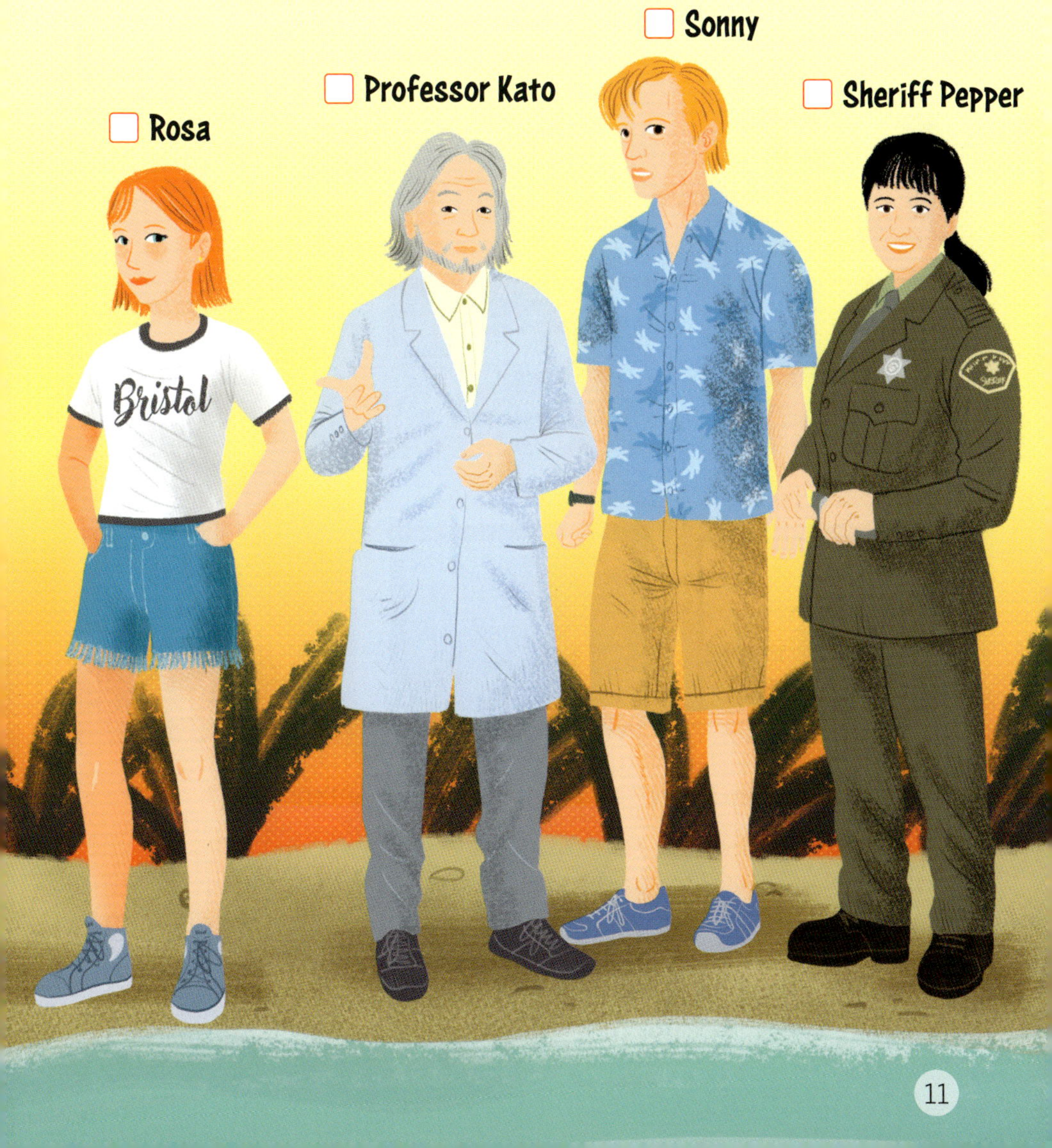

☐ Rosa

☐ Professor Kato

☐ Sonny

☐ Sheriff Pepper

Before Reading

1 **Match the words below to the pictures. Use a dictionary if necessary.**

- ☐ bay
- ☐ bioluminescence
- ☐ coast
- ☐ diving
- ☐ jet-ski
- ☐ seal
- ☐ shark
- ☐ shipwreck
- ☐ surfing

2 **Use words from Exercise 1 to complete the sentences.**

a Mako was attacked by a .... when he was young.

b Can we go diving to see the old ....?

c Along the ...., there was a factory in the middle of the beautiful beaches.

d They jumped on the .... and raced across the bay.

e Midnight Bay is perfect for .... , because there are no rocks.

3 Think of how you say *coast*. Then listen and tick (✓) the words with the same vowel sound (c<u>oa</u>st).

- ☐ boat
- ☐ coat
- ☐ close
- ☐ glow
- ☐ hall
- ☐ know
- ☐ koala
- ☐ saw
- ☐ show

4 Listen to an extract from the story. Then complete the sentences with words from the box.

> glow expert trip amazing few excited about
> waiting Professor outside dressed

California was too hot! She was **a**.................... for the English spring, in jeans and a jumper. She took her jumper off and put it in her bag. She hoped that someone was **b**.................... for her. She looked up and down the line of faces. A **c**.................... people had signs with names on. "Welcome back, Ted!", "We missed you, Mum". Nothing with "Rosa Daniels".

She went and sat on a bench **d**.................... . She was very tired, but very **e**...................., too. This was her first **f**.................... to America! And an **g**.................... opportunity, studying sea animals on a summer exchange programme. Awesome! Her friends were so jealous. Plus, it was a chance to work with **h**.................... Kato! He was an **i**.................... on bioluminescence. She knew everything **j**.................... his work. It was really interesting – animals that could **k**....................!

5 Think about the following questions.

- **a** Where does Rosa live?
- **b** If you could go to another country to study, where would you go and what would you study?
- **c** What makes you jealous?
- **d** What do you want to be an expert on?

6 💬 Share your answers with a friend.

Before Reading

1 **Listen, then choose the correct answer to the questions.**

a Where is Sonny's mother from?

☐ 1

☐ 2

☐ 3

b Where does Bull work?

☐ 1

☐ 2

☐ 3

c What would Rosa like to be?

☐ 1

☐ 2

☐ 3

d What sport does Mako like?

☐ 1

☐ 2

☐ 3

2 Read the questions. Listen to Professor Kato and Sonny, then choose the correct answers.

a What did Sonny forget?
  1 ☐ to bring the professor some books
  2 ☐ that he has to collect someone from the airport
  3 ☐ to finish his work at the university

b What time does Rosa's plane land?
  1 ☐ 7:00
  2 ☐ 7:30
  3 ☐ 10:00

c Where does Rosa live?
  1 ☐ England
  2 ☐ Midnight Bay
  3 ☐ California

d What does Sonny need to bring to the professor tomorrow?
  1 ☐ a video of seals
  2 ☐ some books on sea turtles
  3 ☐ his car

e Who sent a video to Sonny?
  1 ☐ Francis
  2 ☐ Professor Kato
  3 ☐ Rosa

3 Listen to Rosa. Take notes, then in pairs see how much you remember.

Before Reading

Think and Predict

1 **Look quickly through the book and answer the questions.**

   a Who are the main characters?
     1 ☐ Sonny and Bull
     2 ☐ Don Montero and Sandra Montes
     3 ☐ Rosa and Mako

   b What does the story talk about?
     1 ☐ love   **2** ☐ holidays   **3** ☐ ecology

2 **Look at these three pictures from the book. Think of a story to connect them.**

3 Share your story from Exercise 2 with a friend.

4 Think about the statement below. Do you agree with it? Why / Why not? Discuss it with a friend.

> Creating jobs for the local community
> is more important than
> protecting the local environment.

1 California

Rosa picked up her backpack from the floor and walked out into the arrivals terminal. It wasn't really a terminal – the airport was too small for that. It was just a small hall. She checked• her phone – there was no free wi-fi here, and roaming• was expensive. She texted• her mum to let her know she was OK. What time was it in England? Were they behind or ahead? They must be seven or eight hours ahead… so… it was 3.15 p.m. back home in Bristol. It felt like a world away•. Car, plane, plane, plane, here. What time did she leave? What day was it?

California was too hot! She was dressed for the English spring, in jeans and a jumper. She took her jumper off and put it in her bag. She hoped that someone was waiting for her. She looked up and down the line of faces. A few people had signs with names on. "Welcome back, Ted!", "We missed you, Mum". Nothing with "Rosa Daniels".

She went and sat on a bench outside. She was very tired, but very excited, too. This was her first trip to America! And an amazing opportunity, studying sea animals on a summer exchange programme•. Awesome•! Her friends were so jealous. Plus, it was a chance to work with Professor Kato! He was an expert on bioluminescence. She knew everything about his work. It was really interesting – animals that could glow!

Her phone beeped. It was a message from her mum, happy to know that she was OK, sending her love, and asking her to take lots of photos! *Well, obviously!*

'Erm... excuse me, Miss?' A voice made her jump.

'Hello!' she said and looked up. There was a young man standing in front of her. He had blond hair, like a surfer, and an old blue shirt. He was wearing shorts and trainers•.

'Can I... help you?' said Rosa. She wasn't sure about this man.

'Are you...' the man looked down at a piece of paper in his hand, 'Rosa Daniels?'

'Oh! Yes! I am!' she said

'Great! Nice to meet you!' The man held his hand out, 'I'm Sonny, the biology teacher at Midnight Bay High School, welcome to our little town!'

Rosa shook his hand and stood up.

'Let me take your bag! I'm so sorry I was late! It was crazy today at the university,' he said. He spoke quickly, like he was in a hurry to finish his sentences.

'The university?' asked Rosa as they walked outside and across the small car park.

'Yes! They help arrange• the summer exchange programme. We're only a small high school, but thanks to the university we can work on some really exciting projects!' Sonny opened the door of an old blue car and put Rosa's backpack• on the back seat.

─┤ **GLOSSARY** ├────────────────────────────

- **arrange:** organise
- **awesome:** great
- **backpack:** bag you carry on your back
- **exchange programme:** course where students study in a different place
- **trainers:** sports shoes

18

'You're going to work from the school's Marine Biology Centre. Actually, it's pretty° big and lots of university students and professors work with us, too. Free help I guess!'

Rosa opened the passenger° door. There were piles° of papers and letters on the front seat. The envelope on the top had the word ZORRO in big letters on it. She picked everything up and put it on the back seat. On the floor of the car were a pair of wet boots and jeans.

Sonny sat in the car and saw her looking in the back.

'Ah! Sorry, it's such a mess°... really busy days with all the research... collecting animals, you know. Lots to do.'

He turned the keys in the car and turned the air-conditioning° on. Music started playing on the stereo. It was an old French song.

Sonny quickly changed it to the radio.

'My mother was French, I listen to her old songs sometimes. Do you want to go straight to your host family°? Or do you want to see the school and meet Professor Kato first?' he said with a smile.

'Oh, I'd love to meet the professor!' said Rosa.

'Not a problem!' said Sonny.

They drove away from the small airport. They were on their way to Midnight Bay.

- **air-conditioning:** system to keep air cool
- **host family:** family she is staying with
- **mess:** untidy area
- **passenger:** person travelling in a car, bus, train but not driving
- **piles:** lots (one on top of the other)
- **pretty:** (here) quite (not as much as very)

19

Listen in 🔊

Sonny and Rosa listen to a news report on the radio. What do they hear? Listen, then do the activities.

1 Listen and tick (✓) the words you hear.

- ☐ businesses
- ☐ busy
- ☐ coast
- ☐ cost
- ☐ keys

- ☐ passenger
- ☐ plankton
- ☐ report
- ☐ rocks
- ☐ science

- ☐ scientists
- ☐ seals
- ☐ song
- ☐ time
- ☐ tides

2 Listen again. How many news items does the news reader mention?

a ☐ 2   **b** ☐ 4   **c** ☐ 5   **d** ☐ 6

3 What is the weather forecast? Tick (✓).

a ☐   b ☐   c ☐

4 Go to HELBLING e-zone to do the activities and get a clue to help you solve the mystery of Midnight Bay.

My clue is ....

2 Midnight Bay

They were driving along the coast• from the airport. Rosa looked out of the window at the Californian scenery. It was beautiful! The sky was an amazing light blue with little white clouds. The road went around a bend• and suddenly she saw it – the sea! It was bright, bright blue, sparkling• in the morning light. It looked so different from the sea around England. Rosa could see high sand dunes• and long rocky beaches stretching• into the water.

'Is there good surfing here?' she asked Sonny.

'Hmm? Oh yeah! Great surfing! Not so easy on this side – too many rocks. But out by Midnight Bay it's perfect. Actually, you're staying at a surf school!' said Sonny.

'I am? I thought I was staying at a student's house,' said Rosa.

'You are! Mako's dad, Bull, has a surf school and hotel.'

'Wait – who?'

'Mako – oh sorry, Alejandro Moreno, and his father, Joe. But we call them Mako and Bull.'

'Oh, right.' *Is there a story behind those names?* Rosa wondered•.

─ **GLOSSARY** ─────────────────────────

- **bend:** turn in a road
- **coast:** land beside the sea
- **dunes:** hills (of sand)
- **sparkling:** shining
- **stretching:** (here) going
- **wondered:** asked herself

'Yeah, they're kind of interesting,' said Sonny. 'They both love sharks! Which is strange, because Mako was attacked by a shark when he was young! He has some awesome scars•!'

Rosa looked at Sonny. *Is there something strange about him?* she wondered. *Or maybe all teachers in the US are like this?*

'Yeah, Mako's not the best of my students, but he's a good kid. He loves being out in the water, with the animals – he doesn't like the classroom so much! Not like you, right? I saw that you're the best in your school! Top• grades!' Sonny laughed.

Rosa didn't say anything. She did well at school, it's true, but she wanted to be out with the animals as well. Her parents didn't like that idea very much. But they didn't stop her applying• for the summer exchange programme. *And next year, Alejandro – Mako – is coming to England to stay with me*, thought Rosa. She looked out at the sun and sea, and thought about life in California. *Is it going to be boring for the American boy in Bristol next year?* She was nervous about meeting him. And his father! Bull! He must be a big, strong man, with a name like that. Rosa thought about her father. He was thin, and not very tall. He was happy in his job as a dentist. He liked gardening and collecting seashells• and old coins• in his free time.

GLOSSARY

- **applying:** asking to be part of
- **coins:**

- **scars:** marks on his skin

- **seashells:**

- **top:** (here) very high

Rosa listened to the music on the radio and enjoyed the feeling of the sun on her face. She was hot and tired, but excited about this trip.

Then suddenly, she smelt something in the air. It wasn't very nice. Sonny saw her face change.

'Oh yeah... bad smell, huh? That's the new factory. It doesn't smell like that all the time, but once in a while there's a smell. But it's not too bad!' He pointed ahead of them.

Along the coast, there was a huge* factory in the middle of the beautiful beaches and sand dunes. One end was glass and silver, while the other was grey and black. The bad smell was coming from there. Big pipes* went from the factory down into the ground by the sea.

'But, it's right by the sea!' said Rosa.

'I know, but they've got a great Environmental* Officer... they're always testing... it's safe... new green technology! It has won prizes. It's great for the local community. Doesn't look so pretty, but brings a lot of good people and money in. That all helps with our research!'

The car passed the factory. Soon, more and more buildings* appeared. They were arriving in Midnight Bay. Sonny drove up to a large building in front of a sports field. There were a few students standing outside talking. They looked worried.

'And here we are! This is the Marine Biology Centre of Midnight Bay High School. The professor is here, he's working with us. We have more space* than the university for the animals.'

Rosa opened the car door and looked up at the building. It looked big and modern.

- **buildings:** places like houses, schools, factories, etc.
- **environmental:** related to nature, air, water etc.
- **huge:** very big

- **pipes:**
- **space:** free places

Listen in 🔊

What are the students saying?
Listen, then do the activities.

1 How many people are speaking?

a ☐ 1   b ☐ 2   c ☐ 3

2 Listen and tick (✓) who says the following.

a 'He wouldn't let me go into the animal room.'

☐ the girl   ☐ the boy

b 'We spent weeks collecting them from all over the bay!'

☐ the girl   ☐ the boy

c 'He was so cute.'

☐ the girl   ☐ the boy

d 'So you think someone wanted to destroy them?'

☐ the girl   ☐ the boy

3 💬 **In pairs look at the sentences in Exercise 2 again. Then listen again and discuss what the highlighted word is referring to.**

ⓔ 4 Go to HELBLING e-zone to do the activities and get a clue to help you solve the mystery of Midnight Bay.

My clue is ....

3 At the School

'SONNY!' shouted a voice. A man with long white hair and a thin beard• was running down the steps of the building.

'Sonny! Get up here now!' the man said. He saw Rosa and stopped running. He tidied• his hair and slowly walked to the car.

'Ah, good morning! You must be Rosa, I'm Professor Kato. Welcome to Midnight Bay! Sorry, can you wait here for a moment? I need to speak to Sonny, alone. Sonny! Come with me!' said the professor. He then turned around and ran back up the steps. Rosa looked at Sonny.

'I, ah, I'm not sure what's happening, but don't worry. I'll be back in a moment!' he said, opening the car door.

Rosa watched Sonny follow• the professor into the building. She sat for a minute or two and then got out of the car to stretch her legs. A boy and a girl were standing on the steps. They were about her age, or maybe younger, 14 or 15 years old. She smiled at them, but they didn't look at her. They were pointing towards the building. *What was happening?*

GLOSSARY

• **beard:**

• **follow:** go after
• **tidied:** put in order

She decided to go and have a look. It was too hot outside. Rosa took her handbag from the car and went up the steps to the open doors. She looked inside, but there was no one there. She walked in. It was like a reception• in a hotel. There were animal models everywhere, and photos of school projects. She stopped. She could hear loud voices coming from a corridor to her right.

Rosa was curious. She walked slowly down the corridor, past empty classrooms. At the end were two big white doors. She pushed one open a little and looked inside. It was a large room with big glass tanks• along the walls, but the tanks were empty. *This is where they keep the sea animals for the research projects*, thought Rosa. *But where are the animals?* In the middle of the room, Professor Kato and Sonny were talking together in Japanese. The professor was pointing at a computer. He looked very angry.

Rosa didn't understand Japanese, but it sounded very serious. She quickly turned around and walked away. *What was happening? Did somebody steal• the animals?*

She went back out into the sunshine and sat in the car. *I'm not going to say anything*, she thought. *Not yet•.*

Sonny came running down the steps and jumped into the car. He smiled.

'Everything OK?' asked Rosa.

'Oh yeah… yeah, sure, fine!' said Sonny. 'You must be tired, let's go to the hotel and meet Bull! What do you say?'

'Sure!' said Rosa. But she had questions.

They drove quickly through the small town towards the sea. Rosa loved it all. It was so exciting to be away from Bristol!

They turned off the road and down a sandy track•. At the end of the track she saw it – Bull's Surf Spot! A beautiful building beside the ocean. It looked old, and there were lots of smaller buildings around it, and lots of surf boards against the walls.

The hotel was on the beach, just a few hundred metres away was the sea! She could see people surfing. A man was walking towards them out of the hotel. He had a mobile phone in one hand, and he was waving• to them with the other. He looked friendly.

'So, here we are!' said Sonny.

- **steal:** take something that is not theirs
- **tanks:** boxes for liquid
- **track:** small road
- **waving:** moving his hand to say 'hello'
- **yet:** (here) at the moment

Listen in))

What is Bull saying on his phone?
Listen, then do the activities.

1 **Listen and tick (✓) true (T) or false (F).**

		T	F
a	Bull knows about the grey seals.	☐	☐
b	Bull thinks that things were bad before the factory opened.	☐	☐
c	Bull is going to talk to Mako.	☐	☐
d	Mako doesn't care about the local animals.	☐	☐
e	Bull wants to work at the factory.	☐	☐
f	Bull can talk to the professor.	☐	☐
g	Bull's daughter Rosa is in England.	☐	☐
h	Bull sees Sonny arriving.	☐	☐

2 **Listen again and take notes about what Bull IS going to do and what he IS NOT going to do.**

Bull IS going to	Bull IS NOT going to
....	....
....	....
....	....

3 **Go to HELBLING e-zone to do the activities and get a clue to help you solve the mystery of Midnight Bay.**

My clue is ....

4 The Blue Glow

Sonny took Rosa's backpack out of the car and gave it to Bull. Bull looked at Sonny but he didn't smile or say anything. Sonny looked a little scared. He got back into the car and waved to Rosa.

'I can take you to school in the morning. Have a good rest! And see you tomorrow!' he said, then drove away.

Rosa looked up at Bull. He was tall, and he looked very strong. He had long grey hair in a ponytail•, and a big tattoo on his arm. He was wearing a necklace – *were those sharks' teeth?* – and a black earring. But when he smiled, he looked very kind.

'Hello, Rosa! And welcome!' he said.

'Thank you, Mr Moreno,' said Rosa, and walked with him into the hotel.

'Oh, call me Bull, everyone does,' he said and laughed. 'How are you feeling? How was your journey•?'

'Long... but... I'm really happy to be here. This place is just amazing. It's like a dream,' she said.

Bull laughed.

GLOSSARY

- **journey:** act of going from one place to another
- **ponytail:**

'Ha! That's good to hear, not everyone around here thinks like that.' He opened the main• door, and Rosa walked into the reception. There were photos of sea animals all over the walls. There was a little desk, some sofas• and chairs, and a TV. A big open door looked out over the ocean! And outside the door was a deck• with chairs, and a table.

'A lot of people your age want to get away from this little town,' said Bull, carrying her backpack up the stairs.

'Oh! But... it's so beautiful!' said Rosa as she followed him. 'And I can't wait• to see all the sea animals that you have here! Especially the famous glowing• plankton• of Midnight Bay! Do lots of tourists come here?'

GLOSSARY

- **deck:** (here) wooden floor outside
- **glowing:** shining with soft light
- **I can't wait:** (here) I'm happy and excited
- **main:** most important
- **plankton:** very small living things in the sea
- **sofas:** large soft chairs for 2 or more people

Bull looked away. 'Yeah, in the past they came, but now with that new car factory, not many people want to surf or visit anymore. Midnight Bay is not going to be a popular tourist town for much longer.' Bull seemed sad.

'Mako's not here right now,' he added quickly. 'You must be tired. Why don't you relax for a while?'

Rosa nodded•, she *was* very tired.

They walked along a bright corridor until they got to room 15. Rosa's age, and the date of her birthday. *That's a good sign*, she thought. 'Here's your room key, and here's the wi-fi password,' he handed• her an old key and a piece of paper. 'Come down for lunch later if you want.'

'Thank you so much!' she said, and closed the door as he left. She sat down on her bed and looked around the room. It was a small hotel room, a single bed• next to a big wardrobe. There was a sink• on one side, and a small desk and chair. There was a big window on her left. She opened it, and looked out over the sea! It was perfect. Then she lay down on the bed, and closed her eyes.

Rosa woke up in darkness! For a moment, she didn't know where she was. Everything was strange. What time was it? She reached for her phone. It was 9 p.m.! And she was very, very hungry. She washed her face, changed into shorts and a T-shirt, and went downstairs.

She could hear a voice in the reception. But no one was there, the voice was coming from a small TV. Rosa looked for Bull, but no one was around. She went out to the deck and sat looking at the sea at night. She was really here! And... was it really... blue lights out in the bay? It was the famous glowing plankton! A soft blue glow followed the waves. It was magical. Rosa walked onto the soft sand and breathed in the warm night air.

- **handed:** gave
- **nodded:** moved her head up and down to say 'yes'

- **single bed:** bed for one person
- **sink:**

Listen in 🔊

What is the voice on the TV saying?
Listen, then do the activities.

1 Listen and decide what the news report is about.

a ☐ the pollution from the car factory
b ☐ the record-breaking colour of the seas
c ☐ tourism in Midnight Bay
d ☐ a surfing competition in Midnight Bay

2 Listen again and write words that match the definitions below.

a people who live in a town or area   ....

b shining   ....

c the up and down movements of the sea   ....

d people who visit a place on holiday   ....

e place where large quantities of things are made ....

f don't think something is important   ....

3 Go to HELBLING e-zone to do the activities and get a clue to help you solve the mystery of Midnight Bay.

My clue is ....

5 A Hole in the Fence

Then she saw the big car factory, up the coast, to her right. Bright electric lights shone° down on the far side of the bay. It looked terrible. Like a big grey monster. In front of her, in the darkness of the sea, were the amazing bioluminescent plankton, slowly moving with the waves. A magical blue glow. She didn't like seeing the factory so close to the sea.

Rosa looked back at the hotel, but she didn't want to go back inside. Not yet. She started walking up the beach. It wasn't long before the smell of the car factory hit° her — it was horrible! Sonny said it was only sometimes, but that was twice already.

Then she heard something above the sound of the waves. SNIP-SNIP-SNIP. What was it? It was coming from near the factory. She walked further up the beach. In front of her was a fence. A big ugly° metal fence across the beach. There was a sign and a light. ZORRO CARS — PRIVATE PROPERTY°!

GLOSSARY

- **hit:** (her) arrived at
- **property:** land or buildings
- **shone:** made light
- **ugly:** opposite of beautiful

She looked around, then listened, but she couldn't hear anything. Then she saw a hole in the fence. She moved closer and pulled back the metal. Now, she could hear someone moving. And then she saw someone – *a man, a boy?* – walking slowly across the sand dunes, dressed in black and carrying a backpack.

Who was it? What can I do? she thought. *Maybe I can go a bit*• *closer. If I see his face, then I can help the police catch*• *him!* She stepped through the fence.

There were lights around the main buildings of the factory, but here it was very dark. The sand dunes went up and down. It was difficult to see much. Rosa walked forward, looking for the person in black. *Where was he?*

She was close to the buildings now. She stopped. *What was she doing?!* Then she turned around to go back to the hotel and... walked straight into the person in black.

'AH!' she said, then she felt a hand over her mouth. She pushed it away and fell back. The person moved forward, and she saw it was a boy! He was about her age, and tall, with brown curly hair. And he looked angry.

• **a bit:** a little   • **catch:** (here) get; find

34

'Who are you?? What are you doing here?' he asked.

'Who am I?! Who are you? I saw you! You cut the fence!' she said, standing up and brushing° the sand from her shorts.

'You're in trouble! I'm going to tell Bull… and you…' she stopped speaking. The boy was laughing!

'You're English! That means you're Rosa. Well Rosa, you can tell my father what you want,' he said.

Father? she thought. *That means…*

'I'm Mako,' he said, and held his hand out. She slowly shook his hand and looked at him.

'You're my summer exchange partner? A thief°!' she said.

'I'm not a thief! The owners of the car factory are the criminals°. Listen, I'm here to take photos of what they're really doing. Then I can show the sheriff°. You can come with me or go back!'

Rosa waited for a second, then she nodded her head. She wanted to find out more. About the factory, and about Mako.

Together, they moved carefully through the sand dunes and closer to the factory. They came to a car park and a big building. She could see two men moving barrels° onto a truck°! What was in them? Mako took some photos. He walked over to a big metal pipe on the ground. There was a grill° on top of it. He opened his bag and took out a glass tube on a piece of string°.

'What's that?' said Rosa.

'I need to get some liquid from this pipe!' said Mako. He reached through the grill and dropped the glass tube down.

'STOP!' a voice suddenly shouted behind them – they turned around, but they couldn't see anything. Bright flashlights were shining in their faces. Was it the police? Two security guards stepped out of the darkness. 'You're coming with us,' they said together.

- **barrels:**
- **brushing:** (here) cleaning with her hands
- **criminals:** (here) bad people
- **grill:**

- **sheriff:** (US) police officer
- **string:**
- **thief:** person who steals things
- **truck:** lorry

Listen in 🔊

What are the guards talking about before they see Mako and Rosa? Listen, then do the activities.

1 Listen and tick (✓) the words you hear.

- ☐ angry
- ☐ argue
- ☐ father
- ☐ guy

- ☐ many
- ☐ money
- ☐ people
- ☐ pipe

- ☐ smell
- ☐ smile
- ☐ try
- ☐ water

2 Listen again and write the answers to these questions.

a How long did we spend filling up those glass tanks with water?

....

b Is he going to do anything about the smell?

....

c But they repaired the pipe, right?

....

3 💬 In pairs, discuss the following:

a Who do you think 'she' is?

b Why does the woman not want to know what is in the pipes?

4 Go to HELBLING e-zone to do the activities and get a clue to help you solve the mystery of Midnight Bay.

My clue is [..]

6 Zorro Cars

The two guards pulled Mako and Rosa up to the main building. They walked past more trucks with barrels on. Some were arriving, and some were leaving.

Mako looked very angry. The security guards had his backpack and camera.

Rosa didn't know what to think. Arrested on her first day in America! *They're going to send me home! No summer exchange. No working with the professor and Sonny. And Mum and Dad are going to be so mad•at me!*

Mako saw that she was worried.

'Rosa... Rosa...' he said, 'hey, don't worry! They can't do anything. They know me and they know I'm right. You didn't do anything wrong,' he smiled at her.

Rosa felt a little better.

The guards took them into the reception, and up the main stairs.

The building was very modern, with high ceilings° and huge glass windows. There were lots of screens showing people working in the car factory. It looked very clean. They came to the top of the stairs. Two big doors were in front of them. One of the guards knocked°.

The door opened, and a young woman came out. She was wearing an expensive suit° and big silver earrings. She had a tablet° in one hand. Rosa could see a photo of an underwater shipwreck on it. The woman quickly turned the screen away from them.

'Miss Montes! We need to see the boss. We caught these two on the property!' said the guard.

'Thanks, guys°. Leave them with me.'

The two guards walked away.

'Good evening, Mako. Nice to see you again! And you have a friend. How nice!' Miss Montes smiled, but she wasn't happy.

Mako and Rosa followed her into a huge office with glass windows that went from the floor to the ceiling. There was a big black desk in the middle and a grey leather° sofa on the side.

There were beautiful photographs of the area on the walls – underwater shots° of animals, a shipwreck, and even a shark.

A large man with a hat was sitting in a big chair behind the desk. He was looking out over the bay.

'Look at it!' the man said. 'Isn't nature amazing?'

'Nature IS amazing, but not when you pollute° it!' said Mako angrily.

Miss Montes pointed at the sofa. The two teenagers sat down. The big man turned his chair around and looked at them.

┌─ **GLOSSARY**

- **ceilings:** top parts in rooms
- **guys:** (informal) people
- **knocked:** hit with his/her hand
- **leather:** animal skin, used for chairs, shoes. etc.
- **pollute:** make water, air, ground, etc. dirty
- **shots:** (here) photos
- **suit:** jacket with trousers or skirt
- **tablet:** small computer

'Now, young Alejandro is it? Back again? This is the third time, huh? And a new friend! Welcome to Zorro Cars! I'm Don Montero, the Director. And this is Sandra Montes, our fantastic Chief Environmental Officer! She studied in Paris, you know! She looks after• things here. Thanks to her, we have a clean environmental record. No pollution at all, and all these prizes...' the man smiled and pointed to some photos on the wall behind them.

This is strange, thought Rosa, *they don't seem to be angry. Aren't Mako and I in trouble•?*

'You're both criminals, and your factory is polluting the bay!' said Mako.

'Calm down, young man!' said Sandra. 'Look! Look out there! Do you see the glowing blue plankton in Midnight Bay? Plankton can't live where there is pollution. So, there is no pollution! Do you understand?'

Mako didn't say anything, but his eyes were dark and angry.

Don Montero stood up. He was very tall.

'I've called your father, and I understand why you don't like my factory, but we've created jobs for Midnight Bay! Hundreds of jobs! Your father's hotel is in trouble, I know that. I understand you're angry, and I offered a lot of money to your father for the hotel. He doesn't want to sell it, for now. But...' Don Montero paused for a moment, 'you can't say we're polluting the bay! That's serious. I really care about• this town, don't forget that!'

Mako started to speak but just then the phone rang. Sandra went to the desk and picked it up.

'Your father is here,' she said. 'Next time, I'm going to call the sheriff. Do you understand?'

'We understand!' said Rosa quickly.

'Go home, Mako,' said Don Montero. 'And please believe me, we are helping Midnight Bay!'

- **care about:** (here) love
- **looks after:** takes care of
- **trouble:** difficult situation

ZORRO CARS

What does the advert for Zorro Cars say?
Listen, then do the activities.

1 Listen and complete the following sentences.

a At Zorro Cars we want the world ....

b Don Montero started Zorro Cars ....

c Don's father, Van, taught him ....

d Zorro Cars' technology is ....

e At Zorro Cars we look after ....

2 Listen again and complete the advertisement.

Environmentally _____ cars
to keep you _____ .

**Making the world
a _____ !**

ZORRO CARS

**3 Go to HELBLING e-zone to do the activities and get a clue to help
you solve the mystery of Midnight Bay.**

My clue is ....

7 Photographs

Sometime later, Rosa and Mako sat in the chairs of the reception room back in the hotel. Bull walked around the room. He was so angry he didn't know what to say.

'Don't move!' he said. Then he went out of the room.

'Hey, Rosa... listen... I'm sorry. Thank you for coming with me. I promise° you, it's true. All of it.' Mako took his camera out of his bag.

'They've deleted° the photos, but I took some with my phone, too!'

She smiled at him. She was too tired and hungry to speak.

Bull came back into the room with some sandwiches and fruit.

'Rosa, look at you – you're so tired! It's nearly midnight – that's 8 a.m. in the UK! Here, take these and go to bed. I'll wake you up in the morning, OK? Sonny's going to take you to the school to start your research with the others. Now, I need to talk to my son.'

'Dad...' said Mako, 'it was all me°!'

'I know it was!' said Bull. 'But Rosa, listen, you need to stay away from that factory, OK?'

41

Rosa nodded her head and picked up the food.

'I'd like to eat outside, if that's OK, then go to bed. And... I'm sorry,' she said, and walked out to sit on the deck in the cool night air. Inside, she could hear Bull arguing• with his son.

She tried not to listen to them. She ate her food and sent a voice message to her parents. Then she sat and looked out at the sea. There was still a strong blue glow in the waves. She was surprised, she didn't think it would stay so bright for so long. It must be really special this year.

Mako came out and sat down in the other chair.

'Dad went to bed,' he said, 'and tomorrow I have to clean all the surfboards and the boat. Yay!'

GLOSSARY

• **arguing:** speaking angrily

'Well, your dad probably thinks he has to stop you from going to the factory again!' said Rosa.

'I know! But we know they're polluting the sea! And the fish are all weird•. Strange things are happening all around the bay!' he added.

'The fish? What do you mean? Oh! I forgot! When I went to the school this morning, the glass cases were empty! There were no fish or animals!' she said.

Mako sat up quickly.

'What?! I didn't know that! It's Don Montero! He took the animals because they are sick! We have to go back to the factory, Rosa!'

'Calm down. We don't know anything. I only arrived this morning... please, Mako! I just want to study the animals. I have to work with Professor Kato and Sonny tomorrow.' Rosa picked up her plate from the table and went inside.

'Let me take that!' said Mako, and took the plate from her. He went into the kitchen, and came back with a jug of water.

Rosa was looking at the photos on the walls. There were seals, birds, and lots of underwater shots, too. They were beautiful.

'Do you like the photos?' asked Mako.

'Oh yes, they're beautiful! I love photography. I studied grey seals back home in England. I have some photos like these, too. But not as good,' she said.

'I'm glad you like them, I took them. I want to be a marine photographer. But I'm not so good at school. Sonny will tell you that!'

'You took these? Mako, you're really good!' said Rosa.

'I love this bay. I take photos of this bay and the animals all the time. It's my life! And I promise you... when the factory opened, strange things started happening to the animals. There's something wrong. And I'm going to find out what it is!'

• **weird:** strange

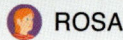 ROSA 🔍 ⋮

Listen in 🔊

What does Rosa say in her voice message to her parents? Listen, then do the activities.

1 Listen and write what Rosa says about the following.

a the journey ....

b Professor Kato's books ....

c why Professor Kato left ....

d where she is staying ....

e Mako and Bull ....

f Midnight Bay ....

g the sea ....

h the next day ....

2 Listen again. Notice the following phrases.

> You know how I love his books!

> It's actually a hotel!

3 💬 With a partner, discuss when you could use the underlined words in conversation. Make dialogues to practise them.

4 Go to HELBLING e-zone to do the activities and get a clue to help you solve the mystery of Midnight Bay.

My clue is ....

8 A Boat Trip

Rosa woke up the next day feeling strange. *Yesterday, what a day!* It was certainly more exciting than England. She got ready and went downstairs. She sat in the small dining room, and had breakfast from the buffet˙ table.

'Rosa!' a voice called from the reception. She got up and went out. It was Sonny, he was there to pick her up.

'Hi! How are you feeling? Did you have a good night?' he said. He was smiling, but it wasn't a real smile. Did he know about last night? About the factory?

'Yes, I'm fine, thank you! I'm looking forward to starting the programme. What's the plan for today?' she asked.

'You're going out into the bay with the professor and some of the other students to get some sea water to test in the lab,' he said.

'Wow!' said Rosa, 'are we going diving˙? I have my licence˙ with me!' Sonny laughed.

'No, I don't think so, not today. And don't fall in the water — there are sharks…' He smiled his false smile again.

GLOSSARY

- **buffet:** meal with a choice of different food that you serve yourself
- **diving:** going underwater (often with air tanks)
- **licence:** document which allows you to do something

'Sharks? That sounds interesting. Are we going near the factory?' she tried to sound like she wasn't very interested, but Sonny quickly turned to her.

'The factory? What? No! Why go near the factory? Did Mako ask you to?'

'I, um, no…! I'm ready! Let's go!' she quickly took her bag, and walked out of the hotel.

Sonny drove through the town, then along the coast and down to a small harbour•. There were a few small fishing boats, and some boats for day trips•. One had "Midnight Bay High School" painted on it.

Sonny turned the engine off, and got out of the car.

'I'm not coming with you today… I have to go back to the school to help with the… umm… with the animals. Look, there's the professor down at the school boat. Have a great time!' Then Sonny turned and got back in the car.

• **harbour:** port; area in water where boats stay • **trips:** short journeys

Rosa ran down to the boat. The professor was moving lots of boxes around the deck•. Three other students were there helping.

'Rosa! Good morning! Meet the other exchange students! They are top of their class, like you! OK. I think we're ready. Let's go, Captain!' said the professor.

The other students introduced themselves• as the captain untied• the ropes and steered• the boat into the bay. It was a beautiful day! Rosa looked out at the waves, and watched the birds following the boat. *How amazing it is to be here!* she thought.

They spent the next two hours collecting water from different places in the bay. The professor was very excited. There was something strange about the water he said, but he wasn't sure what it was.

'We can test it later!' he said. 'Captain! Time to go I think.'

The captain turned the boat around and started the engine. Suddenly there was a POP and a BANG, and they saw black smoke• coming from the engine!

'Oh no!' said the professor.

'What's that?' said one of the students. They looked out into the water, and saw lots of dark shapes• swimming quickly towards them!

Rosa looked closer. They were grey seals•! She laughed. There was nothing to worry about! She loved grey seals.

BANG. A large seal hit the boat! Then another! The boat was moving from side to side, and Rosa fell down on the deck. The other students were shouting.

What was happening? Seals never attack boats!

'Look out, Rosa!' shouted the professor. Another large seal was climbing onto the back of the boat! She could see its eyes were red and it was shaking• its head.

'HELP!' she shouted.

- **deck:** (here) floor on a boat
- **introduced themselves:** said their names
- **seals:**
- **shaking:** moving quickly
- **shapes:** forms
- **smoke:**
- **steered:** guided
- **untied:** (here) opened

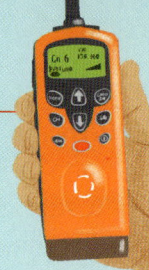

Listen in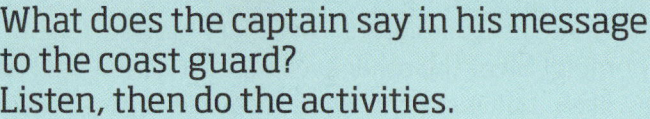

What does the captain say in his message to the coast guard?
Listen, then do the activities.

1 Listen and take notes about what IS happening and what IS NOT happening.

IS happening	IS NOT happening
....	....
....	....
....	....

2 Listen again and complete the coastguard's report.

★ ★

COASTGUARD REPORT

10:00

Boat   ....

Persons   ....

Location   ....

Reason for call   ....

Other details   ....

3 Go to **HELBLING e-zone** to do the activities and get a clue to help you solve the mystery of Midnight Bay.

My clue is ....

9 A Seal Attack

Rosa was lying on the deck. The crazy seal was in front of her. It was looking at her and shaking its head.

'Take the rope!' a voice from the sea shouted. Suddenly, there was a rope next to her! She picked it up just as the other students came and helped her away from the seal.

'Tie it on!!' shouted the voice again. The captain took the rope and tied it quickly to the front of the boat.

The seal was getting closer! Two of the students picked up a pole and tried to push the seal away! But it was too big and heavy.

Rosa ran to the front of the boat – the voice from the sea was Mako! He was on a jet-ski•, he was trying to pull the boat.

Slowly, very slowly, the boat started moving! The engine from the jet-ski was smoking and a huge fountain• of water was coming out from behind it.

The professor and the students were throwing boxes at the seal. Rosa helped, too. She picked up a big box and threw it – BAM! It hit the seal on the nose. Rosa felt terrible.

GLOSSARY

• **fountain:**

• **jet-ski:**

'Sorry!' she shouted to the seal. The seal looked confused, then turned away and jumped off the boat.

All the students and the professor sat down, shocked and tired. The boat was slowly moving away from the seals. The captain came up onto the deck.

'OK! I've got the engines working, but only a little – that Mako boy saved us!' he said.

'Yes, he was great and we're all okay,' said the professor. 'But we don't have the water we collected from the bay!'

Oh no, thought Rosa. *The bay water was in the boxes! And they threw the boxes at the seal.*

'Sorry, Professor...' she said.

'It's OK, I'm glad• we're safe. I don't understand what happened! Seals attacking a boat!'

Rosa looked out at Mako on his jet-ski. He knew something about all this. She had to talk to him. Just then, another boat appeared. A police boat! The police boat threw a bigger rope down to the captain. He untied Mako's rope and tied on the new one. Mako's jet-ski went off towards the beach. The Midnight Bay High School boat was moving quickly now, and soon they were back in the harbour.

─┤ **GLOSSARY** ├──────────────────────────────

• **glad:** happy

A short lady in a police uniform[•] jumped off the police boat and came to speak to them. She had friendly eyes and long dark hair in a plait[•].

'Are you all OK?' she asked. 'I'm Sheriff Pepper and I'm glad we found you! Accidents[•] at sea can be dangerous[•]!'

'Accidents?' said the captain, jumping off the boat. 'It wasn't an accident! I'm sure of that! Someone tried to stop us out there.'

He held up a piece of metal and a black box. Everyone looked at it.

'What is that?' asked the sheriff.

'I don't know, but I know my boat and these are not part of it! They were on my engine. Someone put them there!' said the captain.

'Why, Captain? What were you doing?' asked the sheriff.

The professor answered the question. 'We were taking water from the bay to test. So, you tell me, Sheriff. Who is worried about what's in the water?' he asked.

'Don't start talking about the factory, Professor!' said the sheriff, as she took a plastic bag out of her jacket. She took the piece of metal and black box, and put them in the bag.

'I know you don't like the new car factory, but I'm sure this was an accident, that's all. Let me check these things out, you take these poor students home, OK?'

She looked at Rosa.

'You're the girl staying at Bull's place, right?'

Rosa nodded. 'Yes. I'm Rosa.'

'OK, Rosa, why don't you come with me? I want to speak to Bull, so I can give you a ride[•] to the hotel.'

Rosa followed the sheriff to her car. *What was happening in this little town?*

- **accidents:** bad things that happen but that are not planned
- **dangerous:** that can hurt
- **plait:**

- **ride:** journey
- **uniform:** official clothes for school, work, etc.

Listen in))

What does Professor Kato say to the students?
Listen, then do the activities.

1 Listen and take notes. What does Professor Kato say about:

Midnight Bay

The sea animals

The local wildlife

2 Listen again and answer the questions in pairs. Give reasons for your answers.

a Do these things usually happen in Midnight Bay?

b Are the students going to stop studying science?

3 Go to HELBLING e-zone to do the activities and get a clue to help you solve the mystery of Midnight Bay.

My clue is ....

10 At the Hotel

Rosa sat in the front of the police car as they drove the short distance back to Bull's hotel. Her first time in a police car! *First time for many things*, she thought.

'So, you're from England, right? I'd love to go to Europe! Especially France. My dream is to visit Paris!' said the sheriff. She was very friendly now.

'Umm... Yes... Sheriff...'

'Sheriff Pepper,' said the police woman.

'Yes, Sheriff Pepper,' replied Rosa. She didn't know how to talk to the police.

'Oh, call me Louise! We're like one big family here in Midnight Bay!' said the sheriff. 'Now, what do *you* think happened out there, Rosa?'

Rosa thought about it.

'Well, it's like the captain said... we collected water from different places, then suddenly the engine stopped. And then the seals attacked us! It's so strange. Seals are usually afraid of humans. I don't understand it at all. What could change their behaviour•?' said Rosa.

GLOSSARY

• **behaviour:** way of acting

53

'Change their behaviour?'
asked the sheriff as they turned into the sandy track down to the hotel.

'Yes. I'm not an expert, but I study seals. A mother seal fights for her baby, her pup... or two male seals fight about a female... but they never come onto boats! And that seal's eyes were red. It's like there was something in the water,' Rosa was thinking as she was speaking.

'Something in the water! Oh, honey•, this is Midnight Bay! We have the cleanest beaches and the cleanest water in California — and even the cleanest car factory! Don't you go saying anything like that or I'm gonna• have to put you in jail•! Hahaha!' the sheriff laughed, but Rosa didn't think it was funny.

She stopped the car and they got out. Mako and Bull were waiting for them. Mako ran to Rosa.

'Rosa! Are you OK?' he said.

'Yes, yes I'm fine... you saved us! You were amazing. How's your jet-ski?' she asked.

Mako took her arm and moved her outside onto the deck. The sheriff and Bull were talking inside.

'Forget the jet-ski! What about you? What happened out there?' he said.

'It was crazy! The engine stopped and then these seals attacked us! One jumped on the boat! It had red eyes and was shaking its head.

But what were you doing there?' said Rosa.

Mako looked back to make sure that the sheriff wasn't listening.

'I was testing the water, too. I've noticed that animals in that area of the bay are going crazy so I decided to test the water. Do you believe me?'

Rosa nodded her head.

'I do now! But why that area? Is there anything there?' she asked.

'There is an old shipwreck underwater. I want to go down there. It's dangerous to dive alone though, and my dad won't go with me. He doesn't want to believe me. If people think there are chemicals in the water making animals crazy, no one will come to the hotel!'

'I can dive!' said Rosa.

'You can?'

'Yes! I have my diving license with me. We can go together!' She was very excited.

'It's going to be dangerous... are you sure? We need to go back out there soon, while it's still light. The sharks like to eat when it's getting dark. And I don't have enough flashlights. And... we can't tell my dad. They might send you home if you do this,' Mako looked worried.

Rosa thought for a moment. There was so much happening, but after seeing the crazy seal today, she wanted to do something.

'It's OK. I believe you, Mako. We have to find out what's happening here. Let's do it.'

Just then, the sheriff and Bull came outside.

'Thank you, Mako!' said the sheriff. 'You did a great thing today. But... be careful! No more adventures.'

'Oh no, Sheriff, no more adventures,' said Mako with a smile.

Listen in 🔊

What do Bull and the Sheriff say?
Listen, then do the activities.

1 Listen and tick (✓) who says the following.

a 'Things like this never happened.'
☐ Bull ☐ the sheriff

b 'Wild animals do wild things.'
☐ Bull ☐ the sheriff

c 'Are you joking?'
☐ Bull ☐ the sheriff

d 'You know it, I know it.'
☐ Bull ☐ the sheriff

e 'I'll do my job.'
☐ Bull ☐ the sheriff

2 Why does Bull say there is something in the water.
Listen and tick (✓) two reasons.

a ☐ People don't swim and surf every day.

b ☐ The seals have never behaved like this before.

c ☐ The smell from the factory is very bad.

d ☐ Someone took the animals from the school.

3 Go to HELBLING e-zone to do the activities and get a clue to help you solve the mystery of Midnight Bay.

My clue is ....

11 The Shipwreck

The sheriff went to her office in town to study the black box and piece of metal from the captain's engine. Bull went into town, too. He told Mako he had something important to do.

This was their chance. No one was at the surf school today. Mako prepared the things they needed for scuba diving and Rosa checked the underwater cameras. Rosa sent a message to a friend at home. She wanted someone to know what she was doing in case there were any problems. It was a hot day so they both put on sun cream, then they carried everything down to the boat. It was a small dinghy•, perfect for a diving trip. Rosa and Mako didn't speak – they worked as a team to get everything ready. They knew what they were doing.

GLOSSARY

• dinghy:

Together, they started the little boat up and went out into the bay. It was mid-afternoon now and the sun was very hot. They had some food and drink and chatted• for a while like old friends. *It's easy to talk to him*, thought Rosa.

Mako checked the GPS• on his phone. They were close to the shipwreck. He threw the anchor• over the side of the boat and looked around. There were no seals or any animals that he could see. Far away on the coast, they could see the car factory and the little town.

They put on their wetsuits and checked everything carefully. Time to go. They jumped off the boat and into the water. They cleaned their goggles• and checked everything was working. They only had about 30 minutes of air, and there was a lot to do.

Mako made the OK sign with his hand. They went down and into a new world.

GLOSSARY

- **anchor:**

- **chatted:** talked

- **goggles:**

- **GPS:** (Global Positioning System) position

It was a beautiful blue under the water. They could see for a very long way. Rosa followed Mako down, almost to the floor of the sea. They swam along, above pale coral* and dark rocks. There were fish of all sizes and colours swimming around them. *This is amazing!* thought Rosa. Then Mako turned and pointed ahead. There it was! The shipwreck!

The old metal ship was lying on its side. Parts of it were broken and it was brown from years in the water. They swam in closer and closer. Mako went inside the ship through an open door on the deck. Rosa followed. There! A red light was flashing! They looked closer. There was a plastic box with a tube and a red light. And then further inside the ship, two bigger metal boxes with ZORRO CARS in black writing on the side. Mako moved a wheel on one of the metal boxes. Bright blue liquid came out of the tube! And it was glowing! Rosa and Mako looked at each other. They understood – the bioluminescent plankton, the famous glowing blue plankton of Midnight Bay – was not real!

Mako took lots of photos and then it was time to go back up to the boat. Suddenly, they saw the red light beeping faster. More and more of the glowing blue chemical was coming out of the machine. They tried to stop it but they couldn't move the wheel! Something was happening to the fish around them. They were moving their heads and swimming quickly towards the shipwreck. And now there were bigger fish coming, too!

Mako gave a thumbs up* to Rosa. They had to go to the surface* – now! Rosa didn't look back, she swam after Mako and kept her eyes on him. They weren't very far down, but they had to go up slowly. It was dangerous to go up too quickly. Rosa felt something go past her legs! *Maybe it's a shark!* She kicked back and it moved away. They swam up and up until they got to the boat. Mako got on first, then pulled her up and they both fell back, exhausted*.

- **coral:** hard pink or red living thing that is found underwater and is formed by sea animals
- **exhausted:** very tired
- **surface:** top of the water
- **thumbs up:** OK sign (with thumb)

Listen in))

What does Rosa say in the voice message to her friend?
Listen, then do the activities.

1 Listen and tick (✓) the main reason why Rosa sends the message.

   a ☐ Because she wants to plan a holiday with her in Midnight Bay.

   b ☐ Because she wants her to know what she is doing in case
something happens.

   c ☐ Because she wants to tell her what is happening in the bay.

   d ☐ Because she wants to tell her about Mako and Bull.

2 Listen and match the words below.

a ☐ sea	**1** factory
b ☐ surf	**2** diving
c ☐ scuba	**3** animals
d ☐ car	**4** hotel
e ☐ blue	**5** plankton

3 Think. Why does Rosa send a message to her friend and not
to her parents? Is this a good idea? Share ideas with a friend.
Record a message for Rosa, giving her some advice.

**e· 4 Go to HELBLING e-zone to do the activities and get a clue to help
you solve the mystery of Midnight Bay.**

My clue is ....

12 Don Montero

Back at the hotel, Mako was angry. Very angry.

'I knew it!! I knew it!' he said. 'Zorro Cars polluted the bay! And then they put glowing chemicals in the water to make it seem clean!'

'It certainly looks like that...' said Rosa.

'And... and... they stole the sea animals from the Marine Biology Centre! Because the chemicals are in the animals!'

'Yes, I think you're right,' said Rosa as she sat on the sofa.

'And we can prove• that it's true! We have the photos!' He picked up his underwater camera. 'We need to send them to the sheriff, and the professor, too!' Mako ran over to the reception desk and took out a laptop.

He lifted his camera, took out the card and put it in the laptop.

'You're right, Mako. And we need to tell your father. Where is he?' said Rosa.

'I... I don't know. He went into town but that was a while ago. OK! Photos sent! Oh no... wait...' he said.

'What is it?'

Mako was looking at the laptop.

GLOSSARY

• **prove:** show (that something is true)

'It's my dad's email...he's... he's going to sell the hotel to Don Montero!! We have to stop him!' Mako picked up the phone and dialled a number.

'No answer! We have to go to the car factory before it's too late!' Mako ran out of the hotel.

'Mako! Slow down! How are you going to get there?' shouted Rosa.

'Jet-ski of course! Are you coming?' he shouted back. *What can I do?* thought Rosa. *I'm part of this now!* She picked up a couple of lifejackets and ran to join Mako. They jumped on the jet-ski and raced across the bay to Zorro Cars.

They hid the jet-ski behind some rocks, then climbed quickly over the sand dunes until they got to a small building. It had windows high up in the wall. Mako stood up on tiptoe• to look inside.

'I can see animals!' he said. 'They're testing sea animals in that building! I knew it!'

'Get down!' whispered• Rosa, 'someone's coming...' They hid behind a small dune as a door in the building opened.

A man came out. Rosa couldn't see him clearly, but he was wearing shorts and trainers and whistling a song.

They watched the man go into the main building. There were guards outside the building, and people in the big reception room.

'Our clothes are wet!' said Rosa. 'We can't just walk in.'

'I think we can!' said Mako, and stood up. He looked around then quickly went into the building with the animals. He came out carrying two long white lab coats!

'Ha! Brilliant!' said Rosa. They put on the coats, and walked to the main building.

The security guards didn't look at them. The man at the reception desk smiled at them. They walked across the room and up the main stairs. At the top, they could see the big doors of Don Montero's office.

Just as they were about to open the doors, a voice shouted behind them!

'STOP!'

They turned around. It was the sheriff! And she was with the professor!

'Mako! Rosa! Why am I not surprised to see you here?' said Sheriff Pepper.

'You can't stop us, Sheriff! We need to speak to my father!' shouted Mako. Everyone was looking at them now.

The sheriff and the professor ran up the stairs.

'I'm not here to stop you,' said the sheriff, 'but I think we all need to have a good talk.'

She opened the door to the office, and went inside. The professor, Rosa and Mako followed.

Don Montero was sitting behind his desk. Bull was about to sign a piece of paper. Sandra and Sonny were sitting together on the sofa.

'STOP!' shouted Mako.

'What's happening?!' said Bull.

Rosa stepped forward.

'I think I can tell you exactly what's happening. Zorro Cars is polluting the bay.'

'What?!' Don Montero stood up. 'You don't know what you're talking about, Miss! When I was young, I had a dream. A dream of having my own company. My father worked 10 hours a day but he always had time to help me with my homework. I remember that old car my dad had in the garage... I remember how he didn't have time to fix• it, he spent his time with me... so I learned and I studied and I fixed that car. And from that day I promised to make good cars, the best cars. To make jobs and to keep our world clean. Zorro Cars isn't polluting anything!'

'Mr Montero,' said Rosa, 'I'm sorry, but you're wrong. Zorro *is* polluting the bay and someone here knows why.'

GLOSSARY

• **fix:** repair

After Reading

1 Why is Zorro Cars polluting the bay? First, write your clues below.

2 Now look at the pictures and choose two people who know why Zorro Cars is polluting the bay. Tick (✓).

3 💬 Now tell a friend, explaining why.

4 Listen and check. You can also read the final chapter on the HELBLING Media App.

After Reading

1 Listen and choose the correct answer to each question.

a Who asks Rosa a question?
- **1** ☐ the professor
- **2** ☐ Mako
- **3** ☐ the sheriff

b Where does Sonny want to work?
- **1** ☐ at Zorro Cars
- **2** ☐ at Midnight Bay High School
- **3** ☐ at Midnight Bay Airport

c Who made the glowing chemical?
- **1** ☐ Sonny
- **2** ☐ Sandra
- **3** ☐ Professor Kato

d Who does the sheriff arrest?
- **1** ☐ Don Montero and Sandra
- **2** ☐ Sonny and Don Montero
- **3** ☐ Sandra and Sonny

e What are Professor Kato and Don Montero talking about?
- **1** ☐ how to stop the pollution of Midnight Bay
- **2** ☐ how to make the boat trips less dangerous
- **3** ☐ how to solve the mystery of the glowing plankton

f How does Bull want to celebrate?
- **1** ☐ with a beach party
- **2** ☐ with a visit to Bristol
- **3** ☐ with an English breakfast

2 Listen to the author, Gavin Biggs, talking about *Midnight Bay*. Then choose the correct answer.

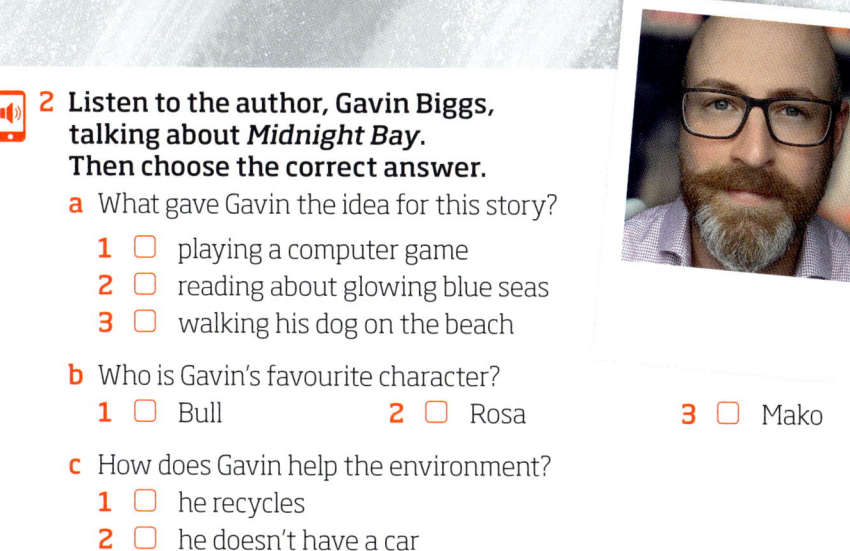

a What gave Gavin the idea for this story?
 1 ☐ playing a computer game
 2 ☐ reading about glowing blue seas
 3 ☐ walking his dog on the beach

b Who is Gavin's favourite character?
 1 ☐ Bull   **2** ☐ Rosa   **3** ☐ Mako

c How does Gavin help the environment?
 1 ☐ he recycles
 2 ☐ he doesn't have a car
 3 ☐ he lives in the countryside

3 Listen again. Then answer the questions with a friend.

a Where is your dream place to visit?
b Do you do anything to protect the environment?
c What does Gavin mean about a balance between danger and excitement? Do you agree with him? Why/Why not?

4 In pairs, answer the following questions. Give reasons for your answers.

a Who was your favourite character?
b What was your favourite chapter?
c Do you think Sonny had a choice about working with Sandra?
d What did Bull mean when he said:

> I think some things are going to change around here, and for the better!

5 In pairs, think of some ways you can help your local environment. Share your best idea with the class.

After Reading

Vocabulary

1 **Complete the word groups with the words from the story.**

boat trip captain coastguard dinghy ~~environmental officer~~ fishing
fishing boat jet ski jet skiing marine biologist marine photographer
scuba diving security guard surfboard surfer surfing
underwater camera wetsuit

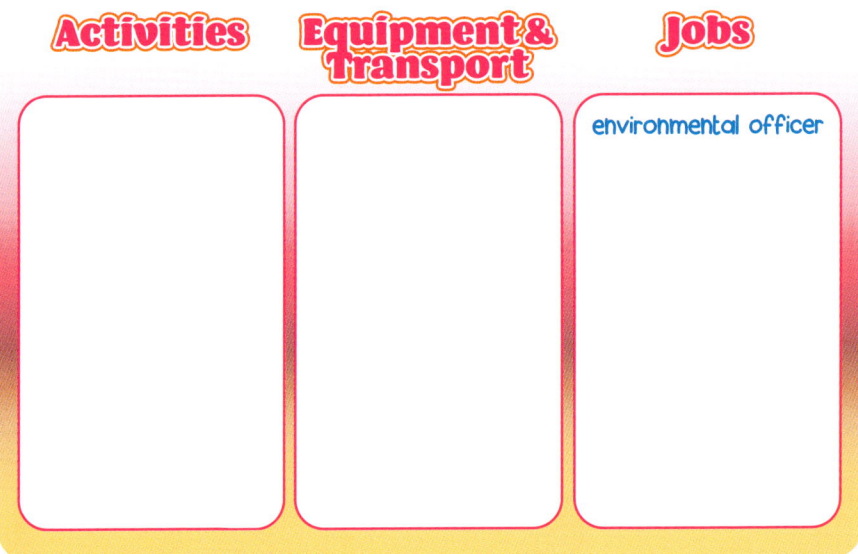

Activities

Equipment & Transport

Jobs

environmental officer

2 **Complete these sentences with some of the words from Exercise 1.**

a It was a small ...., perfect for a diving trip.

b The .... turned the boat around and started the engine.

c 'I'm glad you like them, I took them. I want to be a ....'

d He had blond hair, like a ...., and an old blue shirt.

e 'We can prove that it's true! We have the photos!' He picked up his
....'

 3 **Listen and check.**

The noun *surf* refers to the white tops of the waves when they are near the coast. The verb *surf* means to ride on these waves using a *surfboard*.

4 Listen to its pronunciation. Then repeat the sentences.

   a She could see people surfing.

   b No one was at the surf school today.

5 Which of these words have the same sound as the vowel sound in surf?

   a ☐ could   **e** ☐ never

   b ☐ first   **f** ☐ person

   c ☐ girl   **g** ☐ student

   d ☐ just   **h** ☐ world

6 Listen and check.

7 Complete the descriptions from the story with words from the box.

> beach building hair plankton song

   a brown curly   ....

   b amazing bioluminescent   ....

   c big modern   ....

   d long rocky   ....

   e old French   ....

8 💬 **Choose two of your own adjectives to describe the words below.**

   a .... factory

   b .... shipwreck

   c .... seal

After Reading

Characters

1 Answer the questions with the name of a character.

Bull

Don Montero

Mako

Professor Kato

Rosa

Sandra Montes

Sheriff Pepper

Sonny

a Who has a shark's tooth necklace? ....

b Who is offered a new job as a Science Officer? ....

c Whose family live in Bristol? ....

d Who wants to buy Bull's hotel? ....

e Who wants to be a marine photographer? ....

f Who is an expert on bioluminescence? ....

g Whose dream is to visit Paris? ....

h Who studied in Paris? ....

2 In pairs, find evidence in the story to support the statements below. How do we know that...

- Mako is worried about pollution?
- Rosa knows a lot about seals?
- Rosa doesn't trust Sonny?
- the Sheriff loves her home town?

3 Who says the following? Match the quotes to the characters in the box.

> **1** Bull **2** Don Montero **3** Mako **4** Professor Kato **5** Rosa
> **6** Sandra Montes **7** Sheriff Pepper **8** Sonny

a ☐ Nature IS amazing, but not when you pollute it!

b ☐ Seals are usually afraid of humans.

c ☐ We've created jobs for Midnight Bay! Hundreds of jobs!

d ☐ My mother was French, I listen to her old songs sometimes.

e ☐ Here's your room key, and here's the wi-fi password.

f ☐ Be careful! No more adventures.

g ☐ There is no pollution!

h ☐ Meet the other exchange students! They are top of their class, like you!

4 Look at the quotes in Exercise 3. In pairs, discuss these questions.
- Where are the characters when they say these things?
- Who do they say them to?
- Why do they say them?

5 What do you think? How are Rosa and Mako similar? How are they different? Discuss with a partner.

After Reading

Language

1 **Complete the adverbs with the missing vowels.**

_ ngr _ ly	c _ r _ f _ lly	sl _ wly
q _ _ _ tly	q _ _ ckly	cl _ _ rly

2 **Complete the sentences with the correct adverbs from Exercise 1.**

a The woman .... turned the screen away from them.

b In the darkness of the sea were the amazing bioluminescent plankton, ... moving with the waves.

c 'Nature IS amazing, but not when you pollute it!' said Mako ....

d They put on their wetsuits and checked everything ....

e The professor and Don Montero talked .... together.

f A man came out. Rosa couldn't see him ...., but he was wearing shorts and trainers and whistling a song.

3  **Work with a partner. Say the sentences below in different ways. Choose from the adverbs in Exercise 1. Your partner has to guess how you said them.**

4 Write the past simple of the verbs below.

a catch ....

b come ....

c drive ....

d hear ....

e lie ....

f speak ....

g stand ....

h swim ....

5 Listen and check.

6 Complete the sentences with the correct verb from Exercise 4.

a Sonny .... up to a large building in front of a sports field.

b 'We .... these two on the property!' said the guard.

c Then she .... something above the sound of the waves.

d The door opened and a young woman .... out.

e He .... quickly, like he was in a hurry to finish his sentences.

f Then she .... down on the bed and closed her eyes.

g Mako .... up on tiptoe to look inside.

h They .... up and up until they got to the boat.

7 Use the past continuous to complete the sentences with the correct verbs from the box.

> come do look point sit talk wear

a Rosa .... at the photos on the walls.

b He .... shorts and trainers.

c The professor .... at a computer.

d Professor Kato and Sonny .... together in Japanese.

e The voice .... from a small TV.

f 'What .... (you)?' asked the sheriff.

g Sandra and Sonny .... together on the sofa.

After Reading

Plot

1 What happens in the story? Put the sentences in the correct order.

1	2	3	4	5	6	7	8	9	10	11	12
f											

a Rosa and Mako borrowed some white lab coats.

b Rosa saw the car factory for the first time.

c Mako and Rosa went scuba diving.

d The sheriff gave Rosa a ride in her police car.

e The sea animals were missing from the glass tanks.

f Sonny met Rosa at Midnight Bay Airport.

g Bull gave Rosa her room key and the wi-fi password.

h The captain found some unusual items on his boat engine.

i A grey seal attacked the school's boat.

j Rosa met Mako.

k Sandra Montes said there was no pollution in Midnight Bay.

l Bull and Mako had an argument.

2 Listen and check.

3 Look at the chapter titles on page 3. In pairs, talk about why they have these titles. Choose another title for each one.

> Chapter 4 is called *The Blue Glow* because it is the first time Rosa sees the glowing blue plankton.

> My new title is *The Glowing Plankton.*

4 Answer the questions below.

Why...

a is Rosa excited about working with Professor Kato?

b is Bull sad that there are fewer tourists in Midnight Bay?

c did Mako want liquid from the factory pipe?

d were there wet boots and jeans in Sonny's car?

e did Sandra Montes hide the photo of the shipwreck from Mako and Rosa?

f did the seal attack the boat?

g was Rosa surprised about the seal's behaviour?

h did Mako take photos of the shipwreck?

5 Pollution is one of the themes in the story. Work in pairs to answer the questions.

a In what ways can a car factory be a pollution problem?

b How can Professor Kato's work help Midnight Bay?

c Why is the pollution in Midnight Bay a problem for Mako? Why is he angry about it?

6 What are these things, and why are they important in the story? Share ideas in pairs.

a b c

7 In the story people talk about keeping Midnight Bay 'clean'. What does this mean? Decide with a partner.

8 Think about where you live. Is there pollution? What type of pollution? Discuss with a partner.

After Reading

1 Listen to the conversation between Rosa and Bull. Discuss the questions in pairs.

   a What is Bull holding? Who does it belong to?

   b Where are they?

   c What does Rosa think is beautiful?

   d Who wants to leave Midnight Bay? Why?

   e Who doesn't come to Midnight Bay anymore? Why?

   f When was Midnight Bay more popular?

   g Why is Bull sad?

2 Rosa wants to find out more about the new car factory. In pairs, think of some questions for Rosa to ask Bull.

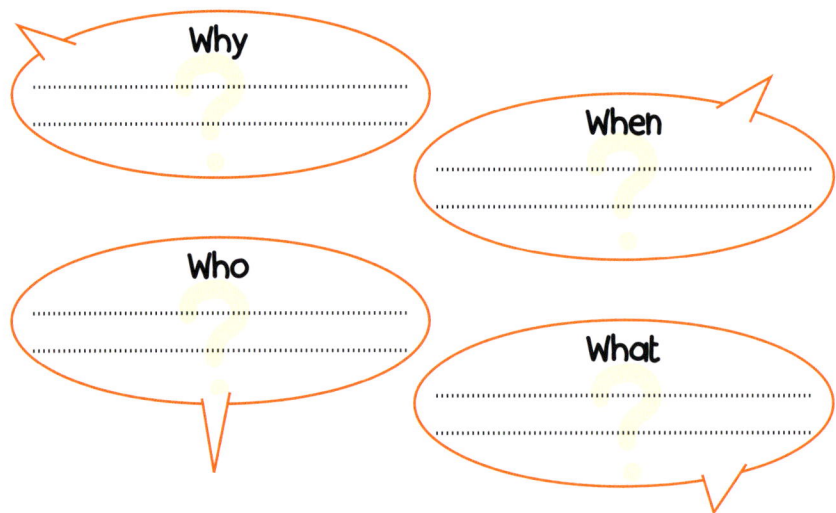

Why ....

When ....

Who ....

What ....

3 With a partner, choose some of your questions from Exercise 2. Role play a conversation between Rosa and Bull.

4 🗨 **Listen to the extract from the story. In pairs, decide which clue below relates to the extract.**

a

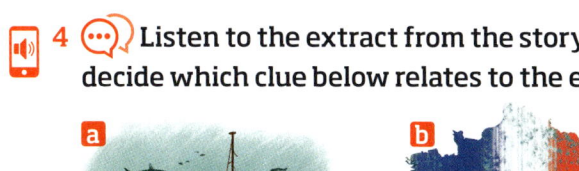
b

c

d

e

f

g

h

i

j

5 🗨 **Talk about the images from Exercise 4 in pairs.**

- What are they?
- Why is each clue important?
- Do they tell us something about Sonny or Sandra? Or both?

6 🗨 **Listen to the extract again. Discuss the questions in pairs.**

a Where are the characters in this part of the story?

b What is inside the glass tanks?

c Why is the professor angry? Is Rosa angry?

d Why did Rosa decide not to say anything?

After Reading

Listen in 🔊 **and Debate**

 A

activist
someone who tries to cause social or political change through their actions

Mikaela Loach is a young British **climate activist** who spends all of her free time fighting to save the planet. When she was a teenager, Mikaela suffered from climate anxiety, and she couldn't sleep because she was so worried about the future. Then she decided to become an activist. She changed her habits. She became vegan and stopped buying fast fashion. But she decided to do more. Now she makes climate documentaries and has over 100,000 followers on her social media channels. 'No one is going to save us,' says Loach. 'Our governments are not going to save us. The only people that can save us are ourselves.'

Can young people make a real difference to the environment?

📱 **1** We asked this question to four teenagers. Who agrees? Listen and tick (✓).

 **1** David  **2** Solomiia  **3** Marcos  **4** Tamara

📱 **2** Listen again and write the correct names.

a .... says that it is not fair to ask young people to change things.

b .... says that young people can ask their parents to help the environment.

c .... says that governments don't listen to young people.

d .... says that if lots of young people change, then they can make a difference.

3 Think. Who do you agree with?

WHAT ARE FOSSIL FUELS?

Fossil fuels are made from dead plants and animals. They can be found deep inside the Earth. Oil, natural gas, and coal are all fossil fuels. Using fossil fuels causes climate change.

 4 What are fossil fuels used for? Tick (✓) below, then share ideas with a friend. Listen and check.

- ☐ To grow our food
- ☐ To heat our homes
- ☐ To make our cars and buses go
- ☐ To make electricity
- ☐ To make some medicines
- ☐ To make mobile phones
- ☐ To make plastic
- ☐ To make power for industry

What are the problems with fossil fuels?

5 Read, then complete the text with the missing words.

global warming
non-renewable
pollution

- They are .... They took millions of years to create and we have already used a lot of them.
- Burning them creates carbon dioxide which keeps the heat from the Sun in the Earth's atmosphere. This is one of the causes of ....
- They cause .... to the air, ground and water, and harm wildlife.

 **DEBATE**

6 In two groups, discuss the question below. Do you agree? Say why, or why not. Give reasons and examples. Use the quotes to help.

Can young people make a real difference to the environment?

I AGREE
GRETA THUNBERG
(Activist)
"I have learned you are never too small to make a difference."

I DISAGREE
ARNOLD SCHWARZENEGGER
(Actor and politician)
"Combatting climate change requires collaboration with many levels of government."

After Reading

Cambridge English Exams

K A2 Key English Test Reading and Writing Part 4

1 **Read the extract from the story.**
  Choose the correct word for each space.

They drove quickly through the small town **1** ....
the sea. Rosa loved it all. It was so exciting to be away from Bristol!

They **2** .... off the road and down a sandy track.
At the end of the track she saw it – Bull's Surf Spot! A beautiful
building **3** .... the ocean. It looked old and there were
4 .... of smaller buildings around it, and lots of surf
boards against the walls.

The hotel was on the beach, **5** .... a few hundred
metres away was the sea! She could see people surfing. A man was
6 .... towards them out of the hotel. He
7 .... a mobile phone in one hand and he was waving
to them with the other. He **8** .... friendly.
'So, here we **9** ....!' said Sonny.

1 a over	**b** towards	**c** between
2 a turned	**b** jumped	**c** saw
3 a next	**b** beside	**c** behind
4 a lots	**b** many	**c** much
5 a exactly	**b** just	**c** simply
6 a surfing	**b** walking	**c** going
7 a has	**b** had	**c** having
8 a smiled	**b** talked	**c** looked
9 a were	**b** are	**c** going

2 **Listen to the extract from the story. Choose the correct answers.**

1 Where are they?
a ☐ Zorro Cars
b ☐ Bull's Surf Spot
c ☐ the Marine Biology Centre

2 Where were the sea animals stolen from?
a ☐ the Marine Biology Centre
b ☐ Zorro Cars
c ☐ the sea

3 Why is Mako angry?
a ☐ Because they found proof that Zorro Cars was polluting the bay.
b ☐ Because his father isn't at home.
c ☐ Because Rosa doesn't agree with him.

4 What is special about Mako's camera?
a ☐ it can take photos in water
b ☐ it glows at night
c ☐ it is smaller than his hand

5 What does Mako need the laptop for?
a ☐ to send photos
b ☐ to look for photos
c ☐ to delete photos

6 Who does Mako think should see the photos first?
a ☐ the professor and the sheriff
b ☐ his father and the professor
c ☐ the sheriff and his father

K A2 Key English Test Reading and Writing Part 6

3 **Write a text message (25-30 words) from Rosa to her friend Lucy.**
In the message:

say you are well.

tell her what happened.

say when you are coming home.

After Reading

 1 **Listen and tick (✓) the correct picture.**

a 1 ☐

2 ☐

b 1 ☐

2 ☐

c 1 ☐

2 ☐

d 1 ☐

2 ☐

2 🇰 **Read and complete with 1, 2 or 3.**

a The sheriff gave Rosa a ride in her ....
  1 dinghy   **2** police car   **3** fishing boat

b Midnight Bay is famous for the .... plankton.
  1 glowing   **2** chemical   **3** surfing

c The captain found a piece of .... and a black box on his boat engine.
  1 glass   **2** sand   **3** metal

d Sandra Montes is the .... Officer for Zorro Cars.
  1 Marine   **2** Science   **3** Environmental

e Mako and Rosa put on .... because it was a hot day.
  1 lifejackets   **2** wetsuits   **3** sun cream

f Rosa was .... about meeting Mako.
  1 scared   **2** nervous   **3** angry

g The photos .... that Zorro Cars polluted the bay.
  1 promise   **2** pretend   **3** prove

3 💬 **Look at the picture on page 26. Ask and answer questions about it.**

What is the professor feeling?

What is Sonny thinking?

What can Rosa hear?

Glow
in the dark

1 **WEB** In the story we learn about bioluminescent plankton. Many other living things glow with bioluminescence. Choose one group from the list below and research it.

> fungi   fireflies   jellyfish   glow worms   squids   deep-sea fish

2 Then choose <u>one</u> glowing animal from your group. Write a Fact File about it. Include the following information:

- common name
- scientific name
- type (e.g. insect)
- size and appearance (what it looks like)
- diet (what it eats)
- lifespan (how long it lives)
- threats (what can hurt it)
- a fun fact

3 Find pictures online to add to your Fact File.

4 Share your project with the class.